Power Packed Book Marketing

Sell More Books

Wendy H. Jones

Published by Scott and Lawson

Copyright © Wendy H. Jones, 2016

www.wendyhjones.com

All Rights reserved. No part of this publication may be reproduced, stored or transmitted in any form, or by any means electronic, mechanical, or photocopying, recording or otherwise, without the prior permission of the copyright owner.

Cover Design by Cathy Helms of Avalon Graphics LLC

ISBN: 978-0-9930677-6-1

DEDICATION

To all those authors who have helped and supported me throughout my journey as an author

To all authors who work tirelessly to write the books which bring so much enjoyment to readers everywhere

ACKNOWLEDGMENTS

Adrianne Fitzpatrick for encouraging me to write this book and for working with me to bring the design to fruition.

Chris Longmuir who has always been confident of my abilities when it comes to marketing books. Also for her patience, help and support in formatting my books.

Contents

	Page Number
Chapter 1: Marketing: An Introduction	3
Chapter 2: Types of Marketing	8
Chapter 3: Keep it Professional	10
Chapter 4: Branding	12
Chapter 5: Start Simple	15
Chapter 6: Book Launches	20
Chapter 7: Website	25
Chapter 8: Book Promotions	29
Chapter 9: Free Promotions	36
Chapter 10: Mailing Lists	40
Chapter 11: Blogs	46
Chapter 12: Social Media	52
Chapter 13: Advertising	65
Chapter 14: The power of the crowd	75
Chapter 15: Keywords	81
Chapter 16: Author Pages	85
Chapter 17: Podcasting	87

Chapter 18: Public Speaking 93

Chapter 19: Short tail versus long tail promotion 96

Chapter 20: Where in the World 98

Chapter 21: What now 103

Chapter 22: Recommended Resources 106

Chapter 1

Marketing: An Introduction?

Why Buy this Book?

You may be a first-time author and new to marketing your book. Or you may have been an author for some time and your marketing efforts are going nowhere. This book is here to help you. It is designed to get you off to a flying start or to give you a boost up to the next level.

This book will provide simple, tried and tested strategies to help you with marketing your own book. These are strategies which have helped me. You can use them as they stand, or you can use them as a springboard to develop your own marketing ideas. Some of the chapters will contain exercises. It is advisable to use these exercises. They will assist you in moving your own Power Packed Marketing Plan forward, right now.

How to use this book

You can either read the book through from cover to cover and get cracking. Or you can dip in and out of it to give you some ideas in the areas where you might struggle. Whichever way you do it I suggest you use the exercises. They are there to get your creative juices flowing. Yes, marketing can also involve some level of creativity. As you complete the exercises let your creative mind fly loose and go wild. Think of the craziest things you could do in each section, and then decide which of these you will put into practice. You'll find marketing and promotion can be fun.

What is Marketing?

In its basic sense, Marketing is getting your book seen by the people who like and want it. In other words it is letting readers know your book is available. However, it is also so much more than that. It is about using as many different formats as possible to get your book seen by as many different types of reader as possible. You need to be aware of who your customer is and what his or her needs are. In order to sell books you need to get inside the head of the customer and market in a way which will reach out to them. It is human nature to think that the only methods which will work are those ones to which you personally respond. However, the bottom line is, you are not trying to sell the book to yourself but to others. Each reader will respond to a different approach. As Joanna Penn states in her excellent book Successful Self Publishing: How to Self Publish and Market Your Book, marketing is about tapping in to the emotional reaction of your readers. You need to appeal to the emotions of your readers in any way you can. This is what will sell books.

What Marketing is Not

It is not spamming the heck out of everyone and everything. This counts in both the real and the online world. You are a person not a writer. Just as those with other jobs are people, not police officers, plumbers, lawyers or teachers. Yes, being a writer is a part of who you are but not the whole. You need to connect with individuals not just shout "buy my book" from the rooftops. If people are interested then genuinely talk about your book. If not, talk about something they *are* interested in. Leave the books aside. They may be interested one day, or they may not. Treat people as individuals not potential readers or customers.

Why Market?

Your book is not going to sell if no one knows about it.

It is generally accepted in marketing circles that for a customer to buy a product they have to have seen it six or seven times. This means they have to have seen your book cover six or seven times. Readers may be reticent in shelling out good money for a new author. The more they see a book cover and blurb, the more likely they are to buy.

Think about this question for a few minutes:

Are you an author, business man/woman, or both?

I am hoping the answer to this question is both. However, writers are often shy and retiring by nature and many don't like the marketing aspect of the process. This may be how you feel. But, to misquote a phrase, this is not the time to hide your book under a bushel. If this is what you do, then that is exactly where your book will stay. No one can buy a product they have never heard of. I am sure the fact that you have bought a copy of this book means that you are serious about moving your marketing forward.

Exercise

1. Buy a notebook you will use for your marketing ideas.

2. Write down what you are already doing.

3. Identify what has been effective.

4. Write a pros and cons list of marketing.

If you have not yet done anything to market your book, then there is no need to panic. The best time to start marketing your book is right now. You cannot do anything about the past but you can do a lot to change the future. If you are about to start writing your first book then the good news is, the time to start marketing your book is right now. Yes. That's right, the minute you write the first word. Tell people that you are writing a book and generally what it is about. This means the genre not the whole plot from A to Z. As the book progresses give updates. This will build a buzz and readers will be ready for the book to launch.

Whilst you are reading this book I would like you to be thinking about the different ways in which you can implement these strategies into your own life right now. You should be thinking about how these could fit into your own marketing arsenal. If they do not exactly fit what you require think about how you can adapt them to your needs.

Chapter 2

Types of Marketing

Chris Syme has written an excellent book called Smart Social Media for Authors. In it she identifies three types of marketing, - paid, owned and earned. Within this there are a veritable plethora of strategies. This chapter will give an overview of each, and outline some of the different strategies which will be covered in this book. There may be some crossover between these.

If you are going to market effectively using all available channels then you will need a marketing budget. Now this doesn't have to be the size of the GDP of a large country, or even a small one, but you will need a budget. I appreciate that many writers have little money to spare so initially you may want to focus on the methods which are free or extremely low cost. However, it is worth saving some money towards the cost of paid marketing. Think of what you can give up to put towards this. It doesn't have to be a lot, maybe the cost of a coffee each week, but saving shows commitment to your marketing plan.

Paid marketing includes: paid advertising, fliers,

posters, postcards, banners, and renting stalls at book and local fairs and events.

The clue is in the name for this next one. Owned marketing is advertising you personally own and can control. The biggest of these will be your website. There are many sites which offer free website builders and you may want to start off with one of those. However, if you want your own domain then a paid website is the way to go. I will discuss this later in the book, in the chapter on websites. Other owned advertising methods are social media accounts, blogs, newsletter, email list, podcast, postcards, posters etc. As you can see, there is some crossover between owned and paid.

Earned marketing can come under the banner of social sharing. This type of advertising includes guest blogging, interviews or guest spots on podcasts, book recommendations from readers or bookshops, book reviews and sharing on social media. Never underestimate the power of this form of marketing. In many ways it can be the most powerful tool you can use. It is also the main one over which you have no control.

Each of these, individually, will help sell your book. However, taken together they can form the basis of a power packed book marketing plan and help you to sell more books.

Chapter 3

Keep it Professional

The first, and most important, part of your marketing strategy is to make sure that your book is professionally designed and produced. If you are traditionally published you may have little control over this. However, if you are an independent author you will and you should make sure you approach it as a professional.

The saying, 'you can't judge a book by its cover', may be true, however readers *will* judge your book by its cover. If a cover doesn't suit, a prospective reader goes no further. You should take the time to look at examples of book covers in your genre. What sort of covers do the best selling books have? What is their design like? It is worth employing a professional cover designer. In fact I would go so far as to say it's a must. Unless you are a professional cover designer, turning your hand to writing novels, this is not the time to go it alone. The same applies to editing and your professional photograph.

Yes this will cost you money. However, you should bear one thing in mind. You are not only an author writing books, you are also running a business. It is worth investing in your business and this is the first step in that investment. People are spending their money investing in your book. They expect to have a professional product in return.

As well as having a professional approach to your book, you yourself need to come across as professional in whatever you do. This applies equally when you are at book signings, on social media and when anyone gives your book a bad review. It also includes being supportive of others be they readers or authors. You are by far and away the most important part of your Power Packed Book Marketing strategy. How you come across to others, both potential readers and other writers, is crucial. This can make the difference between readers buying your books or moving on to a different author. It can make the difference between other authors supporting you or ignoring you. Be pleasant, polite and approachable in everything you do, be this online or in the physical world. In other words, be the author you would most like to meet.

At the same time you need to be passionate. This of course means being passionate about your books, but also means being passionate about your abilities. If you doubt either of these it will come across to potential purchasers i.e. readers and they will not buy. If you do not believe in your product then why should anyone else?

Chapter 4

Branding

Branding is the process of creating a unique name and image for yourself and your product. Once you start to publish, it is what will attract and keep loyal readers. You want readers to think about you, as an author, and your books when they see a certain image. Now I am not advocating you have something like the Nike logo, although you may want to have a logo as part of your branding. There are ways in which you can create your own brand.

The first part of your brand is your author name. Everything you do should be associated with that name. This may be your real name, or another name entirely. My name is Wendy Jones, which is fairly common, so would not stand out on social media or in bookshops both physical and virtual. Therefore I use my middle initial H, making Wendy H. Jones.

Branding also includes the genre in which you choose to write. If you write in two genres you may want to think about having two names. If you are a romance writer and decide to write horror your readers are going to be a trifle confused when they see the genres mixed up. Another part of writing in a genre is that people will know what to expect when they read your book. Therefore you need to find your voice as a writer in that genre.

Cover design should also demonstrate your brand. Your covers should stand up to the quality of your genre, but should also stand out from the rest. My covers all have a scene from Dundee at the bottom of the cover. The top is a scene from the book. Each book has the same theme but different images and colour. Therefore they have a general brand but are distinctive in their own right. My cover designer, Cathy Helms of Avalon Graphics has done an amazing job and I could highly recommend her if you need a cover designed or redesigned. Another designer I would highly recommend is Jessica Bell Author/ Musician/Cover Designer. As you can see, Jessica is a multi talented lady. Both of these cover designers produce high quality covers and work closely with authors to ensure the final results meet their needs.

The main characters of your books are also part of your brand. Readers develop a relationship with a character and are genuinely devastated if that character disappears. You need to write characters who will evoke an emotional response in readers whether it is to love or hate them. I read a series of crime books where the main detective barely had a redeeming feature, and yet I read the books because she was so compelling.

The way in which you set out your table for book

signings is also part of your overall brand, as is the way in which you conduct yourself on social media.

One final note about branding. Your brand should be around you as an author, not an individual book. Series will come to an end but if the reader is invested in the author they will go on to read more series from them. I can tell you all my favourite authors but could not tell you the titles of any of their books. I just know I love the books.

Exercise

1. Spend 10 minutes jotting down what it is you wish to portray in your branding.

2. Think about this over the next week. Give ideas time to take root.

3. If you already have books out consider what the strengths are in your current branding.

4. Is there anything that could be improved?

There are authors who have completely redesigned the covers and titles of their books. They did this because they either felt the branding was wrong, or they wanted a fresh and modern look. I am not saying you should do this, I am saying it may be something which is worth considering in order to make your brand more appealing.

Chapter 5

Start Simple

Writers often have many objections to marketing. They say they are introverts and that is why they write. Often writers feel that they do not have what it takes to be a marketer, that they are not pushy and get embarrassed pedalling their wares. If you feel like this then I understand. You are absolutely right. You may not have the skills required for marketing. Yet. However, what you do have is you. You are a unique individual with your own distinctive skills and talents. Use these to develop your marketing plan. Use them, and mix them with the techniques in this book to develop your own Power Packed Marketing strategies. This is the combination which will work for you.

Consider this. It may be be time for you to change your beliefs. Many authors start with the belief that their nature will not allow them to market, therefore they will not succeed. If this is you then it is time to turn that belief system completely on its head. Start by setting yourself a goal. This may be the number of books you would like to sell in a month, or the amount of money you would like to earn in a month. It may be a goal for the year. Keep that goal in a prominent place. The cupboard above my computer is a good spot for me. Then work out what you can do to help yourself reach that goal. It may be mini steps at first, but then you will take bigger steps as you see the progress you are making towards that goal.

Your First Step

In order to identify your unique talents I would encourage you to do a SWOT analysis. I am sure you know what this is, but for those who haven't yet come across it SWOT stands for

Strengths

Weaknesses

Opportunities

Threats

Strengths

What are you good at? Where do your particular talents lie? An example of this could be that you are a graphic designer. Use this talent to develop knock out book covers. If your strongest talent is writing then apply to guest blog on other people's blogs.

Weaknesses

What are the areas that you feel need to be developed?

Identifying these will help you to move them forward.

Opportunities

What opportunities have you got to market your book? These could include speaking engagements or attending local craft fairs.

Threats

What is going to get in your way? This could be lack of time to write or to market, not having a budget or anything else you think could stop your marketing endeavour.

The following template is usually used to help with this task

Strengths	Weaknesses
Opportunities	Threats

This may be simple but it is powerful. Think about it carefully and answer honestly. It is especially important to be honest with yourself when it comes to strengths. Once you have done so then use the strengths and opportunities to develop the weaknesses and negate the effects of the strengths.

It's about Time

Time! We all seem to have so little of it these days with a million demands seemingly sucking time away. As a writer you may feel that you can barely snatch enough time to write never mind market your books. This is a fair point. I don't know your individual circumstances or what is placing demands on your time. I do know, however, that it is worth carving out a little bit of the precious stuff each day to market your book. There may be a myriad of brief moments where you can use time differently. Here are some examples off the top of my head

1. Sitting in the car waiting for the children to come out of school. Send out a tweet, put a photo on Facebook, or share a pin on Pinterest. These are all things which can be done in seconds on your mobile phone

2. Waken up fifteen minutes early and look up a list of local craft fairs. Find one, which fits in with your schedule, and book a table

3. If you are out buying groceries pop into the supermarket café. Put your feet up, figuratively of course, have a cup of tea and write your blog. This can be done on your phone, no need to be in front of a computer these days

4. If you're out for a walk, take a photo of something interesting and post it to social media

5. Order some postcards of your books

However, it may mean deciding in what way you would like to use your time. You may have to give up watching one of your favourite TV shows and use that time for marketing. It is about choices and the choice is yours.

Exercise

1. Write a SWOT analysis in your notebook.

2. Work out where you could carve out ten minutes a day to devote to marketing. Put these in your diary and stick to them. Make this time protected time for you and your book.

Chapter 6

Book Launches

Book launches can be physical or online. I will take these separately as there are different ways of approaching each.

Physical Book Launch

Having a book launch in a physical book store starts with relationships. This means building up a relationship with the manager and assistants. Buy books, chat to them about what you are reading, and build up a familiarity. They are therefore more likely to be open to your request. The four main bookshop chains in the United Kingdom are Waterstones, Blackwells, WH Smith and Foyles. There are also many independent bookshops. If you are not in the UK, then approach your nearest bookshop or research the main chains in your area.

When you approach the manager of your chosen shop it is important not only to be confident, but also to appear confident when you talk. This is where being passionate comes in. This passion will come across to the manager and they are more likely to grant your request. Take a copy of the book, outline where it fits in with the books already on their shelves. If it is set locally let them know that. Give them a date when you would like to hold the launch. You may have to be flexible as to the date. If you will do anything like provide snacks or food let them know that. Often they will agree then and there. They may wish to get back to you. If they don't get back within a couple of weeks it is acceptable to ring them. However, do not hassle them. You are building a long term relationship with the bookshop so it is important to stay professional.

The bookshop will want an idea of numbers. They are only going to stock your book and hold a launch if they feel it will be financially viable to them. It is down to you to invite people and make the launch go with a bang. I invited everyone I could think of. I also placed fliers in cafes near the bookshops and in the local libraries. I created a real buzz about it on social media and made it into an exciting event. On the night it was packed with standing room only. There was a professional photographer there who did a sterling job of grasping the buzz and capturing it in pictures. Planning your launch is important, but you then need to deliver on the night. Tell the audience about yourself and your writing journey, and read from the book. The questions and answers can be lively and you need to be prepared for any questions or comments.

Once you have done one book launch it is important to change things up for the next one, but also get the same sense of buzz. I talked about the History of Hanging in

Scotland, at one of my launches. I write contemporary books but who doesn't love a good hanging. Of course I write crime books. If you write romance this may not be the best approach to take. This is your opportunity to think outside the box and come up with your own ideas. My first thought for romance writers was the history of Valentine's day. However, as St Valentine was a Martyr who was tortured and beheaded you may want to omit that part of the history.

If it is not possible for you to have a launch at a bookshop then you will need to think about equally exciting opportunities. There is no rule that you have to hold a book launch in a book shop. How about church halls, village halls, theatres, libraries, school halls, coffee shops or restaurants. In fact anywhere that has the space to take you. I brainstormed a few ideas for book launches and came up with these:

Historical - A Cream Tea

Crime - Hold a murder mystery dinner party for charity and launch your book there.

Sci Fi - Dress up as your favourite character.

Romance - dress up as a romantic heroine or hero from the movies, or a book of course

An author friend of mine, Fiona Veitch-Smith, wrote a mystery set between the wars. This was The Jazz Files starring investigative reporter Poppy Denby. She dressed up in clothing from the time, as did many of the guests. Her launch went with a swing in more ways than one. This is a great example of how to make use of your book's topic to build a buzzing book launch.

Online Book Launch

These are approached slightly differently and are usually for ebooks only. Most authors set up an event on Facebook and invite people from their Facebook friends to join the event. Often your friends will invite other people. You can also share the event from your Facebook author page. I will talk about the author page in greater detail later. Online book launches usually include Author Q&A, competitions and prizes. Before the day and time you post on the event and get readers hyped up and ready. When the day arrives you need to be online for the whole period. Some people say all day but I would stick with a period of an hour at a time when your guests are available. If you want this to be international then remember the time differences. It may need to be later in the evening in the UK to accommodate guests from the USA. My advice, as per the previous chapter, is to start simple. Once you have done one event and it is successful then you can build this up.

You will need to prepare in advance what you are going to do to keep the party lively. Use virtual cocktails, or hot drinks and nibbles. Name your cocktails after characters in your books or go with the theme of your book. Anyone for a Killer Cocktail? This goes with the theme of my books which all have the word Killer in the title and all have second word beginning with C. If you're a romance writer, anyone for a Smoochie Smoothy. Okay maybe my attempt at romance is a little off but you get the idea. Remember, my ideas are a springboard for your much more creative and appropriate ideas.

You can also post small extracts from the book. Post teasers from the book. Anything, in fact, which will keep guests engaged and wanting more. Wanting more of your book that is. If your launch is an hour then every 15 minutes or so, post a link to buy the book.

Finally if you do decide to hold competitions keep the prizes small and light so they can be posted easily. Make it clear where you are willing to send the prizes. If you are in the UK it can cost a lot of money to send something to Australia or the USA.

Chapter 7

Website

As I said earlier in the book website builders can be either free or paid. The free ones include

Webs   http://www.webs.com

Wix   http://www.wix.com

Joomla   https://www.joomla.com

Wordpress: https://wordpress.com/create/

Webs and Wix are easy to use drag and drop website builders. You can start simply with these and they will walk you through all the stages. Joomla and Wordpress can be a bit more tricky to use, but are both excellent website builders. You can also get paid options from all of these sites.

You will also need to use a host service. This is the server where the website will sit on the Internet. I use Bluehost, which I have found to be excellent. There is a cost for this each year as you are effectively renting web space.

It is worth buying your own domain name. This is the name by which your website will be known. My domain name is wendyhjones which makes my website http://www.wendyhjones.com It makes sense to use your author name as this is the name you want associated with your books.

A website is one of the few things which you can control completely in your marketing endeavours. Even if every social media site dropped off the face of the earth you can still advertise and promote books on your website. Even if every bookshop, real and virtual, disappeared you can still sell books from your website. Please note, if you are in the UK and wish to sell digital products from your website you need to be clear about the legal aspects of VAT. It may be wise to stick to physical books until you get your head around this.

Unless you are a computer whizz kid it may be better to hand the website building over to someone else. I am fairly computer savvy and it took me quite a number of hours to get to grips with website design. A website is considered a marketing essential, but your time may be better spent on writing more books.

If you do wish to design your own website there are a number of excellent books out there which will help you master this. I am not going to recommend any specific book as the one you buy will be dependent on your level of skill at the starting block.

Your website should contain, as a minimum:

Your newsletter sign up - This can be a popup or static but it should be on your landing page. I will be talking about this in greater detail in Chapter 8

A strong Author Bio

Links to buy personalised signed copies of your books

Links to buy your books from Amazon, iBooks and Kobo

Social media share buttons

Follow buttons to your social media profiles

A page for your blog

Embedded book previews from Amazon - This is a fairly new feature as I write this book. Visitors to your site can preview the books on your site and then buy directly from Amazon. I have also added links to other places that visitors can buy the book

Your Twitter Feed - This allows others to see you as more than just a writer. It lifts you from 2D to 3D proving that you have a life other than writing

Make the most of your website. It is a powerful tool in your Power Packed Marketing arsenal.

One of the most important things to remember when building your website today is the rise and domination of mobile technology. More people are now using mobile devices than desktops or laptops, to browse the

Internet. Google will also give greater placement in rankings to websites which are mobile optimised. This means it is worth spending time and money to make sure your website is fully mobile compatible. Once it has been built, and after you make any changes, check it out on multiple devices to make sure that all pages are loading properly and quickly.

If you are looking for a web designer one I can highly recommend is Simon O'Loughlin of One Off Web http://www.oneoffweb.com/ He is highly professional and takes great care to ensure that he builds websites that completely meet the needs of his clients.

Exercise

1. Take a look at some websites of authors who write in your genre.

2. What do you like about them?

3. What don't you like about them.

4. Jot down some ideas for your own website.

Chapter 8

Book Promotions

This chapter will be covering physical book promotions. Online book promotions will be covered in greater detail later in the book.

Promoting your book can be hard work, but it can also be lots of fun. My experience is that the fun far outweighs the hard work aspect of promotion. You also get to meet a variety of readers, some of whom will buy your book, some who won't. That doesn't matter. They are seeing your books and may buy in the future. They may also tell family and friends about your books. Not everyone will read in your particular genre, but they will know others who do.

Below are a number of places where you can do book signings

Cafes

Shopping centres

Coffee shops

Craft Fairs

Christmas Fairs

Book Fairs

Summer Fetes

Schools - Yes I write crime fiction. However, I was asked if I would like them to sell my books to the parents and donate £1 from each sale to the School funds

Fund raising events - give a proportion of each sale to the charity

Conferences

Libraries

Museums

Re-enactment events - particularly useful if you write historical fiction

Whilst these are primarily about selling books they can be so much more than that. They are also about promoting your book. On your table you should have postcards for each of your books, with the book cover on the front and the blurb and buy links on the back. You can take this one step further and add a QR code. Scanning this will take them directly to the site to buy the book. If visitors say they only read on an ereader, then give them the postcards. The same applies if they say they don't read crime. They may have friends or family who do so will take the cards. Book signings are as much about promoting as selling.

Try to make your table set up as visually appealing as possible. If you just have books it is human nature to think "They're trying to sell me something" and many people will scurry past. Make it appealing and they will stop to chat. When I set out my table I have books (of course), postcards, bullets, a bloodstain, a knife, syringes and a hangman's noose. More about that noose later. I also have some free sweets to give away. The sweets are my secret weapon. If you ask people if they would like a sweet it serves two purposes

1. They notice you

2. They usually stop and chat

This can be particularly true if you are in coffee shops or cafes. If you are sitting at a table with a pile of books many people will walk past. If you ask if they would like a sweet they will take notice. I have many people say to me, "I didn't even see you there. What are you doing?" They have then gone on to buy one or more books. Never underestimate the power of a free Quality Street when considering marketing. By the way I use Quality Street because they are gluten free. Any other sweet will do.

Along with your table being visually appealing it is sometimes worth dressing up yourself. I have done book promotions as Jack the Ripper and Santa Claus. I will admit the Santa outfit was basically a Christmas jumper and a Santa hat. My spiel, "This is your only chance to get your crime book signed by a smiling Santa." I change this to Jack the Ripper for other signings. Some ideas for you could be a suffragette, or the hero or heroine from your book if they are distinctive enough. This may also give you more confidence to engage with visitors as the eyes move from you selling books to your display. Selling books is a pleasant aside to the whole event.

Another writer friend of mine, Dorothy Stewart, wrote a superb book called When the Boats Come Home. This was a historical saga based around the fisher women who followed the herring boats around the country. For one event she dressed up as a fisherwoman. However, Dorothy took this one step further and learned how to gut herring. Now that is what I call dedication and genius. Genius marketing that is. What could you do that is different and will get you noticed?

Any events you do should be well advertised. Put up posters, hand out leaflets, and discuss with the venues how they will promote it. Talking of venues, many are more supportive of writers than you would think. Go in, tell them you're a local author, say why it is linked to that particular venue and ask if you can do a book signing. The worst they can say is no. If they say yes, set a date and time. If they say no, try another venue. I haven't had a venue say no to me as yet. Most are keen as it can bring in extra custom. Also use social media to advertise your event. Tweet about it using an appropriate HashTag. There will be more about HashTags in Chapter 12. Set up a Facebook event and invite people along. When I do an event I also tweet about it and post on Facebook, live from the event. This reminds people that the event is on and may also reach new readers.

Another method of promotion, which is quick, and relatively cheap, is to carry postcards around with you. Hand these out if anyone asks about your books. I buy these from Vistaprint but there are many other places that you can buy these. You may also be able to get them locally and support a local business. Ask local businesses and cafes if you can leave postcards in there. Many are happy to support local enterprises and that is what you are.

Going back to what was said at the beginning of the book. A customer needs to see something 6 or 7 times before they buy. Therefore you need to make sure that you are in as many places as possible. This does not mean you personally but includes personal appearances. It means posters, flyers, events, postcards, bookmarks and anything else you can think of which will get the word out about you and your books.

One fun idea I use is t-shirts. Some authors have these with their books on. Mine merely say:

'Anything you say may be taken down and used in a book'

'You are dangerously close to becoming a body in my next novel'

These make people laugh and start a conversation about your books. They can also be worn at book signings as, again, they will start conversations.

In many cases there will be an initial outlay for book signings. Coffee shops and cafes will usually allow you to do signings for free. I usually buy a coffee or some food. However, tables at Craft Stalls will cost money upfront. As a rough guide I pay £10- £15 per table depending on where the event is being held. Promotional materials such as postcards also cost money. You will also need to buy paperbacks in order to have stock to sell. You should consider this as an investment in your business. You need to make the decision if your business, in this case your books, are worth that investment. I have made the decision to say a firm yes to this, as I want readers to be able to find my books.

Promotions are about getting to know people and them getting to know you and your books. Chat to people in general. If someone says they are buying a book for a birthday present ask them if they would like it signed Happy Birthday or something else. Tell them about your books but if they say they don't read crime don't force it. Ask what types of books they do read and chat about that. They will remember how pleasant you were and might buy your book for someone else when a present buying occasion comes along.

My top tip when attending book signings at craft fares or any other event:

Arrive early and set up before it starts. Do not start to pack up until the end of the event. I have had people buy all six of my books whilst other stalls were still setting up. I have also sold all six copies just before I packed up. If you say you will be there for a specified length of time, you must be there at that time.

Exercise

1. Jot down a list of places you could approach to arrange book signings.

2. Choose 3 of these and approach them today.

3. Research places where you could have postcards made and work out the costs.

4. Jot down a list of local businesses who you think would be willing to take postcards or flyers.

Chapter 9

Free Promotions

There are a number of ways that you can promote your books for free. As an author you may find that you are a member of several organisations.

If you are a member of an organisation use their benefits and services wisely. They provide help, support and access to a number of experts in both writing and publishing. Many of you may be members of the Society of Authors. This includes those of you who are traditionally and independently published. Independent and hybrid authors may also be a member of ALLi (The Alliance of Independent Authors). I am a member of ACW (The Association of Christian Writers), in fact I am their webmaster at the time of writing this book. I am also a member of the Scottish Fellowship of Christian Writers. My books are not in the slightest Christian, but I am a Christian so eligible for membership of these organisations. Each of these provides links to your work on their websites. This includes your books, blogs, websites and often events. The Society of Authors and ALLi have search functions to discover authors to do talks etc. Of course these organisations provide so much more than just advertising your book. However, as this is a marketing book I will be focussing on the marketing aspect.

I suggest that you use these organisations to their fullest if you are a member. If you are not a member then it is well worth exploring membership.

Both ALLi and ACW have a blog, which comes out daily. There are opportunities to be guest bloggers or even regular contributors. This will be covered in greater detail in Chapter 11 on blogging. Again, this is effectively free advertising and a way for you to get your name known in the wider world. However, it is also about supporting others, by providing information that will be of benefit to other authors and readers. Make the most of these opportunities. They are like gold dust.

Joining online groups for your specific genre, or country, is also a good way of getting the word out about new releases. I am not saying everyone in the group will buy your book but they do tend to be supportive. They will also share with others. Please note, like all interaction these groups are not about buy my book. Their primary function is to support members with writing and to celebrate achievements. These include yahoo groups and listserves. Look out for online writer groups and join them. Interact and engage long before you start to tell people about your books. As with everything engagement is the key to selling more books. Once people know you as a person they are more likely to buy or share your books.

You can get free advertising for your events via local newspaper websites. Local newspapers often have free listings for local events in the print version of their newspapers as well. Talking of newspapers, it is worth sending out a press release to local and national newspapers. This may bring sales, or it may not. Opinion is divided as to how effective newspaper articles really are. However, it is another way of getting your name out there. Remember that a customer needs to see a product at least six or seven times before investing in the purchase. It is worth having a press release kit ready to send out to newspapers. This should contain:

Your author bio

Information about your book

The release date of the book if it is a new release

A high resolution, professional photo of yourself

A high resolution image of the book cover

You can also add some sample questions and answers as they may use these as the basis of an interview

Local radio interviews can also help to get your name out to the wider public. Listen to your local radio and identify the programme which has the best fit. This is important as you want to have the best chance of getting airtime. Contact the DJ and outline what you do and how it will benefit local listeners. Let them know you are available for interview. Sending them a copy of the book will give them a better idea of how you fit into their programme. Be polite and pleasant. If you are accepted for interview then take time to prepare. Learn about the show. Listen to several episodes. Learn something about the person interviewing you. This way you will come across as a pleasant and all round person rather than someone who simply wants to flog their books.

Think about other media opportunities as well. I contacted STV, the Scottish version of ITV. For those of you not in the UK this is a television company. They weren't able to interview me for the main news, but they did do an interview for STV online and have continued to do so as each book comes out. This has been viewed and shared a number of times and is getting the word out about my books.

Chapter 10

Mailing Lists

Along with your website your mailing list is one of the few things you can totally control. If every other method of marketing fell apart you would still be able to use your mailing list. Of course if the world's electricity supply died tomorrow it might be slightly trickier. However, that's a story for another day and I can feel a novel coming on.

Back to our mailing lists. As I stated previously it is important that you have a signup for this on your website. It can be either a popup or a static signup, what is most important is that it is mobile friendly. Many people now are doing their entire web browsing on mobile devices. If it does not show up on a mobile then vast swathes of the world's population will not be able to see it. It is worth employing a professional for this part alone, even if you design the remainder of the site yourself. I know this from experience. I was able to add the signup myself and then discovered it would only open on a computer or a laptop. I had to call in the big guns to sort it out. As many people have popup blocker installed on their mobile devices it is worth having both a popup and a static signup. Delay the popup so it does not interfere with what they are reading straight away. Readers need time to invest in the content of your website before being interrupted by a popup.

One of the best ways to get someone to sign up to your website is to give them something free in return for their email address. As a writer it makes sense if this is a book. I have written a new book for this purpose, but it fits in with your overall series image and branding. In my books there is a running theme where DI Shona McKenzie is thinking about ways to kill her boss. Many people said they liked this aspect of the book and found it funny. Therefore my free book is DI Shona McKenzie's Guide to Killing Your Boss. It is a PDF file and can be read on any device including mobile devices. As I only have three books out at the time of writing this book I did not choose to give away the first book in my series. I know many other authors who do. If you are a veteran writer with a lot of books under your belt then this may be something worth exploring. I will be doing so as my portfolio grows.

The wording of the signup needs to entice the reader to buy the book. I have the following on my website

'Shona is feisty, funny, sharp and smart. She also spends a lot of time thinking about how to bump off her boss. Here for the first time she shares her secrets with you in the free book, *DI Shona McKenzie's Guide to Killing Your Boss.*'

Under this are fields for name and email address then a

clickable button saying 'tell me where to send your free ebook now'.

Give the reader a taste of what they are getting but keep it simple. Remember those mobile readers. The more information they have to wade through the less likely they are to click through. Click through is the name of the game when considering email sign up.

Once you have an email list it is worth advertising it to grow it. This will be covered in more depth in chapter 12. You also need to ensure that you send out quality information. This can be about what you are writing, interesting facts about the location where your book is set, information about the characters, writing hints and tips, discussions about books, and last but not least, letting followers know about future book releases. Keep it short, keep it lively and keep it interesting. Readers now have many demands on their time. If they have to spend half an hour reading your email letter then they will not carry on. Especially if this is on a mobile device. However, it is important to make it long enough that you engage the reader. Try it out, see what works, and make changes if necessary. The beauty of this is the flexibility. If it doesn't work, change it until you find out what does work. Each time you try it more readers will sign up.

When it comes to newsletters you will be sending this out via email. The subject line of your email is crucial. The average person in the western world has hundreds of emails dropping into their inbox on a daily basis. The important factor is click through. That is, how many people are clicking on your email and opening it. The title needs to catch the eye, and imagination, if subscribers are to explore further. There are a number of blogs and articles out there which will help you to examine this in more detail.

You should run your email list through email handling software such as MailChimp or aweber. This handles all the legal stuff like keeping addresses private and not spamming people. It allows you to add an unsubscribe option at the bottom of the email. Most importantly it automatically adds anyone who signs up to your mailing list and makes it quick and easy to send out multiple emails. It also gives you data such as number of subscribers and number of click throughs. There is a free version of this which you can use for up to 2000 subscribers. However, this does not have many of the automated features that make it much easier to use. I would recommend signing up to the paid version. If you feel that this is one payment too many then the free version is good.

One of the most useful benefits that you get by using these services is the data they collect. I can see that 72% of subscribers to my list have subscribed via a mobile device. That is almost three quarters of readers who are interested in my books. With statistics like this you can see that it is imperative to make sure that any mailing list activity is fully mobile compatible.

Once you have built your list you can use campaigns to

send out a regular newsletter or contact your subscribers with news of new releases or events. The important part here is do not spam. Use your list wisely and to provide benefit to your subscribers. Use your list to turn casual readers into loyal fans.

Email management companies

MailChimp   http://mailchimp.com

AWeber   http://www.aweber.com

Some people use the lure of large prizes, such as a kindle, to entice readers into signing up for their mailing list. This is false economy and will probably not result in a lot of sales. People will join in the hope of winning the prize and will not be invested in your books. They will probably unsubscribe soon after the competition closes. Mailing lists are about gaining fans, not the largest number of subscribers. It is quality over quantity. If you give away a free book if readers like it they will stay signed up to your list and may buy more of your books.

Exercises

1. Explore both of the above email management companies.

2. Decide what you could use as a free gift to encourage readers to sign up for your newsletter.

3. Choose one and sign up to the free trial today.

4. Do you feel it suits your needs? If so, start building your email list now.

Chapter 11

Blogs

Every writer should have his or her own blog. This is one of the other areas of marketing totally under your control. If you haven't already got a blog then there are some free blogging platforms to get you started. These can be integrated into your website once this is up and running.

Free blog hosting sites

Blogger

WordPress

Wix

Tumbler

Weebly

I find blogger to be the easiest to get up and running. However, you will need to decide which is the best for your needs. The free versions of these sites can have a few limitations but they have enough features for you to have a professional blog.

One point to note, if you are thinking of having a WordPress website, then it may be better to have a WordPress blog. This is not essential, I have WordPress/Blogger, but it may make things easier down the line.

Hints and tips for bloggers

1. Any blog with a number in the title usually gets the most views. This is proven fact as people like to know what they will be learning or getting from reading the blog.

2. Maintain focus but write on diverse topics within this.

For example a writer's blog could contain - author interviews, tips on writing, technology for writing, technology for readers, book reviews, short stories, and book launches among many others. You could also share marketing tips and photos of book signings or book launches. This is a good example of how all marketing works together.

3. Disseminate your blog. This is not the time to hide

your light under a bushel. People won't read it if they don't know it's there.

4. Use pictures in your blogs. Blogs which contain pictures are more likely to be read and shared. Many people are now sharing on Pinterest and this cannot be done without a picture.

5. In order for your blog to gain followers you must:

Write well.

Write often - this does not mean every day unless you want to. However, if you decide to write once a week then keep to the schedule. Readers will lose interest if there are gaps.

6. You can use your blog for marketing your own products. However, be careful not to spam. Treat it like you would any social exchange. Social media, of which a blog is a part, should be 90% social 10% product information. It is perfectly acceptable to put permanent links to your books on the side of the blog

7. Link to your blog on your website and your about.me page

8. Add share buttons for Facebook, Twitter, Pinterest, Google+ etc. to your blog

9. Remember your blog is a showcase for you as a writer. People who read your blog are more likely to buy your books

10. Add a call to action, such as a question which can be answered in the comments. The more interaction there is on the blog the more fun it will be for readers. It will also be more discoverable in online searches.

Your blog can be used to showcase your new releases and is a valid part of your Power Packed Marketing Plan.

Blogging is so much more than writing your own blog and sending it out into the stratosphere. It is also about reading blogs on marketing and keeping up with what is new in the industry. Here are a couple which I particularly like:

Seth Godin   http://sethgodin.typepad.com

Social Media Examiner
http://www.socialmediaexaminer.com

Writer Access   http://www.writeraccess.com/blog/

The first two are not specifically about marketing books but they are excellent and all the advice is transferable.

Blogging is so much more than putting out your own blog. It is also about social sharing and supporting others. One of the ways in which you can do this is to host other writers or marketers on your blog. This can be in the form of interviews, or guest posting. Look out for opportunities to guest post on other blogs within the industry. Very often opportunities will come along when you are not looking and you will be invited along to another blog. These opportunities are golden and you should, wherever possible, grab them with open arms. However, make sure that you are a fit for the blog in the first place. It isn't worth going on a blog about quantum physics if you've written a children's book. Unless your book is about quantum physics for children of course. Okay, I'm being slightly tongue in cheek here, but you get the picture. Some requests can be quirky but a perfect fit. I have been invited to guest post on Shelley Workinger's fabulous FoodFare blog. This is about food in fiction. My post will be on the food they eat in my DI Shona McKenzie Mystery series. Anyone who has read my books will know that Shona and her team eat - a lot. What an exciting opportunity and what a great idea for a blog. If you would like to take a look at Shelley's blog here it is http://bookfare.blogspot.co.uk

Book review blogs are also a good way of getting your work known. There are many of these and they do an amazing job. However, review bloggers are often booked up months in advance. Look for some of these in your genre and reach out. It is important to make sure that the blog is the right fit for your genre. An excellent one for crime writers is Lyndsey Adams 'There's been a Murder'.

blog.https://theresbeenamurder.wordpress.com

Exercise

1. Spend a few minutes looking at reviews of the different blogging platforms.

2. Jot down ideas for the main focus of your blog.

3. Brainstorm some titles and do a search to see if these are already taken.

4. Set aside a couple of hours in your diary to get your blog up and running.

5. Write your first blog.

Chapter 12

Social Media

This section could be turned into a book on it's own. In fact Chris Syme has done just that in her book SMART Social Media for Authors, which I would highly recommend. This chapter will give you a brief overview of the ones I use regularly. It will also suggest some ways in which you can use these effectively to start your own power packed social media marketing quickly and easily.

There are a large number of social media sites out there, and I mean a *large* number. The latest list I could find outlined 176 different sites. It is obvious that no author has time to worry about all of these. You might be thinking not a chance as you read these, and I wouldn't blame you. However, it is important to be on at least some. The main ones are Facebook, Twitter, Pinterest, Linkedin and Google+. Instagram is growing in popularity, as is Vine. It is advisable to be active on at least four of these. If you write Young Adult books then I would recommend SnapChat as this is the site used by those in that age range. Even if an author does not want to be on any of these at the moment I would advise them to register their author names on each of the sites. If your author name has already gone you need to think carefully about what you will use instead. It needs to be professional and allow readers to find you. I was fortunate in that I registered for the sites I use pretty much as they started out. I was also fortunate in that I used my middle initial on these sites long before I started writing. This means my author name was already registered. I am telling you this because it may be as simple as adding your middle initial to register. You may need some lateral thinking here to come up with a solution.

The most important thing to remember when considering social media is that it is called social, and not selling, media for a reason. It is designed to interact with friends, family and fans not flog your products. The balance should be 90% social and 10% about buying books. Long gone are the days where writers could hide behind a screen of anonymity. Fans now expect to be able to interact and get to know more about the authors whose books they enjoy reading. You may not wish to share your life with fans, and for you it will fall into the SWOT threat category. However, seeing it as an opportunity can turn this around. What can you share without giving away every intimate detail down to inside leg measurement?

Social media marketing can be fun. In fact I would go as far as to say it should be fun. It is an opportunity for engagement and conversation, for inspiring and informing, for learning and for teaching, for celebrating and commiserating; I could go on. As you can see it is so much more than selling books. It is about being you, and you will sell books as part of the process. Don't be so desperate to sell books that you forget you are, first and foremost, a unique and exciting person who also happens to write books. As writers we are so caught up in our identity as writers we can often forget the rest of our lives.

Facebook

I am sure you will already be familiar with Facebook. Essentially it is a free social networking site where you can connect with friends and upload video, pictures and links. You can share news and chat with others with whom you are friends. As far as writing and marketing goes there are two ways in which you can interact with readers.

Facebook Author Page

If you are running a business you are not allowed to do so from your normal Facebook profile. If Facebook finds out you are doing this they will remove your profile without discussion. You will then lose all the contacts and friends you had made prior to this happening. They are strict on this and will give no notice before removing your profile. Therefore you must have an Amazon Author Page. You can call this what you want but a simple name followed by author will suffice. Remember it must be a page not a profile.

Your author page is the place to share news about

books, events, cover reveals, new releases etc. However, it is still a place where you have to be social. On my author page I share pictures about what I have been doing both work related and social. I also share interesting facts and photos of Dundee where my books take place. For example, I shared the BBC news item of a theft of a cash (ATM) machine from a shop nearby. The police then caught the thieves at a nearby McDonalds. This was merely a bit of light relief. I have also shared pictures from the Scottish Association of Writers Gala dinner, at their conference. Pictures from Bloody Scotland have also been posted and shared. Who can resist a few photos from a conference with a name like that? It is a crime conference by the way before you think I am slagging off my homeland.

When it comes to your author page interaction is the name of the game. The more likes and comments your posts get the more people will get to see your post. Only about 4% of those following your page will see your posts organically. Facebook is a business and, like all businesses, want to make money. Therefore they want you to advertise to boost your posts. Facebook advertising will be covered in greater detail in chapter 13.

Facebook groups are also a good way of getting the word out about your books. They are also a great way to find new authors and new books to read. Like everything interaction is the name of the game. When you join a group take time to interact and get to know other members. When you do post about your book check back and respond to any questions or comments.

Think of the equivalent in the real world. Would you go in to a group, hand out flyers about your books, talk about your books and nothing else then walk out of the door without letting anyone get a word in edgeways? This is effectively what you do if you dump and run in a Facebook group. However, one caveat, do not thank everyone who likes your post. This bumps your book up to the top of the group page again and is considered bad manners. Use groups wisely. Do not post the same thing to a hundred groups in one day. This will just clog up your friends' notifications and they will lose the will to live. Or at least the will to remain friends with you on Facebook. There are also a number of groups which are purely for learning and supporting each other. These are superb and worth their weight in gold. I am a member of several of these and have learnt so much from other writers. The most useful one I have found is that belonging to the Alliance of Independent Authors. There is usually a no promoting your book rule in these groups.

One of the ways in which I use Facebook, and indeed all my social media platforms, is to show pictures of my books on bookshop shelves, myself at book launches or book promotions or signings, or anything else to do with your book. These go down well and are a good way of getting the word out about your books without saying buy my books. They should, however, be interspersed with social sharing.

Twitter

I am sure that many of you reading this book are already using Twitter and are familiar with the site. For anyone new to this, Twitter is a microblogging site where you have 140 characters to impart your deepest thoughts in a tweet. This can then be retweeted (shared) by others. The idea is that you follow people and read their tweets. These often contain links which can take you to articles, author websites, places to buy books or other items, or any other site on the World Wide Web. They often have photos attached. You can use this site to get the word out about new releases, reduced price books, 'cover reveals' or any other photo which you feel will be of interest to your followers.

When starting on Twitter many people do not grasp how it works, or how useful it can be. This is because they are following few others and have no followers themselves. As a writer start by looking for other writers in your genre and follow them. Then you will get an idea of how it is generally used by writers. However, Twitter is so much more than that. You can follow people with many different interests and tastes. Follow people who may be writing about the areas you need to research for your novels. Send out tweets yourself. Make them interesting and informative and people will start to follow you back. This is when it starts to get interesting.

In order to use Twitter you need a Twitter Handle. This

is how people will be able to find you. Funnily enough mine is @WendyHJones. My advice is to use your author name unless it is already taken. If it is, think again, but remember not to be too weird and wonderful. If you want people to find you and see you as a professional writer, @FluffyBunny may not give the right impression.

HashTags are also important when using Twitter. A HashTag is the symbol # followed by a word which then signifies the topic of your tweet. Anyone searching for that HashTag will see your tweet. If you are looking for HashTags to market your books, blogs etc. then here are some, which I have found useful. As a guide you should use no more than 2 HashTags per tweet.

#Iamwriting

#Amwriting

#Writing

#Editing

#1lineWed (one line from your book with book link - it works)

#Writingwednesday

#AmEditing

#AmReading

#WritingTips

#writinginspiration

#writingprompt

#writerslife

#readingispower

#author

#authornews

#booklaunch

This is just a quick guide to help you get started. However, my little list pales into insignificance compared to this ultimate list of HashTags for authors. If you type this into your browser you will enter a veritable Aladdin's Cave of HashTags:

http://www.bookmarketingservices.org/ultimate-list-of-author-specific-hashtags/

There are many tweet groups where authors band together to retweet each other. These can be good but use them sparingly and use discretion. If you never mention diet or food in your tweets, and the only books you mention are crime, your followers are going to wonder why you are suddenly tweeting about a book on the cucumber method of dieting. Okay I made that up, but it is usually obvious you are a member of a tweet cartel. You do not want to put your followers off, as they will start to unfollow you.

Social media can be a time suck and authors often find that they spend far too much time on there. In frustration they start to automate everything they do. My advice is do not do this. If you follow someone on twitter and they immediately send you a private message saying thanks for the follow here's a link to my book, website, amazon author page or Facebook page, this is a sure indication they are using an automated service. If you do this then you will find yourself losing followers faster than you can say unfollow.

Twitter Chat

This is another excellent use of Twitter. I have been involved in a few of these and I have organized one myself. This can be a really good way of interacting with fans, other writers and those interested in your genre. There are a few simple steps before doing so.

1. Find two or three other authors in your genre, and invite them to join the chat

2. Arrange a date and time when you are all free. Remember to allow a few days to advertise the event. If you want to chat to the International, then you need to remember the time differences. The one I am doing is at 9 PM GMT. This allows readers and writers in the USA to join in the chat

3. Advertise the event widely using social media. All writers who are involved should contribute to the advertising

4. Where possible advertise using graphics as this will catch the attention

5. Make sure you communicate clearly with all those taking part. Tell them when you expect them to be available for the start of the event

You can take this even further. One of the authors involved in my event, Fiona Veitch Smith, suggested that we could have a prize for the best question. This was a copy of one book from each of the authors. We would then ask the winner to post pictures of themselves with the books on social media. This leads to increased advertising for the books

You can also advertise on Twitter and again this will be covered in chapter 13.

Pinterest

This is basically a way of pinning photos and articles on online pin boards. Other users can either follow you, or each of your individual boards. These can be about anything you want them to be. I have a number of Pinterest boards including - Social Media Marketing, Writing, Books and Reading, Mystery Writing, Forensics, Literary Quotes, Gluten Free Food,

Penguins, My Dundee, Scone Palace and Stirling amongst many others. Yes, you've got it. Pinterest is all about social sharing and being supportive of others. You can share other people's pins and people will follow you if you pin things which are of interest to them. They will also repin your pins. So how can Pinterest help me to market I hear you ask? There are a number of ways in which this can be done.

Book board - just for your books, covers, links to buy, interesting articles about the area in which they are set. Interesting articles about the period in which your books are set. An example of this would be pictures of clothes set in the time period of your book. This is particularly suited to Historical Fiction but a little bit of thought will mean you can use this for any time period.

Interest boards - If your character rides a Harley Davidson then a board on Harley Davidsons would be perfect. Any boards which would be of interest to your readers. So if you are writing romance a board on Valentine's Day, or romantic Christmas gestures. I write crime hence the reason I have a forensics board.

Book link boards - These could contain the pages of all your books on every platform on which they are available. This should be the only specifically buy my books board you should have.

You can have secret boards which you and only those

invited can see. Now before you think I am suggesting anything dodgy here, I am not. I have a secret board only I can see. In there I keep research for my books. My cover designer and I have a secret board for sharing possible cover images.

Google+

This is another social sharing platform this time run by Google. You can add people to circles and they can add you to their circles. This is pretty much like following on other sites. You can also join groups and set up groups. If there is something you are interested in there will be a group on Google+ for it. Again it is important to be social and interact with others. This way others will interact with you. Then they are more likely to respond when you post about your books.

One of the features, which I like the most on Google+, is, Google Hangouts. These can be messaging, voice or video calls or a mixture of these. They can be useful for doing a single author talk and those attending can ask questions. I have been involved in a couple of these where someone in the USA has interviewed me about my work and my books. Prior to the Hangout you can invite people along, using all the social media platforms. At the appointed date and time you go online and start to chat. You can talk about what you are doing and answer any questions that come in. These sessions can be recorded and then placed on YouTube. It is therefore useful to also have a YouTube channel. Managed properly Google hangouts can generate a lot of buzz and interest.

As you can see there are a diverse number of ways in which you can use Social Media effectively. This is, on the whole, free advertising so use it well. Don't waste the opportunity by spamming everyone in your friends list. Use it to have fun, enjoy yourself, and entertain and support others. In the process you will sell books.

Exercise

1. If you are new to social media register your author name on the five major ones.

2. If you are already using social media use some others which you could use to develop your social media marketing.

3. Connect with others in your field on the different social media sites.

4. Look out for Twitter chats and join in the conversation. This will help you to get your name out there as someone who is supportive and interested.

5. If you have been using twitter for some time identify some authors and invite them to join in a twitter chat.

Chapter 13

Advertising

Much of what I have been advising so far is free or low cost. However, if you are serious about selling more books then you will, at some point, have to use paid advertising. There are a number of sites out there which offer paid advertising. This can cost anything from a few dollars to over a thousand dollars. I can't tell you which ones to use, or guarantee they will work for you. However, I will outline a few of these so that you can explore them further. You need to make the decision as to how much you are willing or able to spend on paid advertising.

BookBub

This is the platinum level of advertising. The number of subscribers varies from 200,000 to over 3,5 million depending on the genre you write. Therefore the costs vary depending on genre. As a crime writer it informs me there are 3.5 million subscribers and I could expect 3,660 paid downloads. However, they do not guarantee this and the advertising costs at the time of this book going to print are $480 for a free book - $2400 for a book which costs $2 and up. This is if you advertise to all regions. This cost drops if you advertise to selected regions. The USA is still high with the cost being topped at $1900. The top cost for UK is $275. I do know authors who have had good returns from this and have sold thousands of books. However, as I say this is not guaranteed. I have not tried this yet but I fully intend doing so. Please note, not all books put forward for a place on BookBub will be accepted.

Books Go Social/The Book Promoter

This is an excellent site run by Laurence O'Bryan. This is not a one day promotion but a long term one for up to a year. It costs anything from $59 - $249 depending on the level of promotion you would like. This involves daily tweets for one to six weeks, a daily email to their subscribers, and inclusion on the website You need to be willing to reduce the price of your book for the period of the promotion. I did a mid range promotion with them and have been very pleased with the results. My sales were strong for the period of the promotion and have continued to be strong over the following two months. There are also two Facebook groups which go alongside this. These are very well run and are supportive and helpful.

This company also offers a featured author promotion. I have just signed up for a two months with them as a featured author. I have done so because I was impressed with their professionalism when I did my initial promotion. They are supportive and answer questions promptly and efficiently. Just a few days in to this I am pleased with the results. There has been a noticeable uptick in sales, not only on the promoted book, but also on the other books in the series. This service comes with several extra features. These include tweets of your cover graphic several times a day, and a single book email advertising your book. However, your book needs to meet certain criteria before it can be accepted for the email advertising. They will also interview you as a featured author. From my results so far I would say that this is well worth exploring.

I would highly recommend this company for advertising. However, remember that sales cannot be guaranteed with any promotion that you do.

Ereader News Today (ENT)

This is a well-established company and is highly recommended by many authors. Again prices vary with genre and the price of the book you are advertising. However the most you will pay is $130 at the time of this book going to print. They do have a large number of subscribers and their email list is popular with readers.

The Artist Unleashed

This is the blog of writer Jessica Bell. She is also the cover designer recommended above. This style of advertising is slightly different in that you create an advertising banner which stays on the side of her blog for a month. The advertisement links to your Amazon author page or any other page of your choosing. This costs $40 - $80 per month, depending on the size of the advert. This is an excellent blog with a wide readership and advertising here is a good way of getting your work in front of readers. I am currently in the process of arranging advertising with the Artist Unleashed. I would like to add that I have found Jessica to be helpful and extremely professional.

The Fussy Librarian

This is another well established site. They have around 124,000 subscribers, and will add you to their newsletter on the date of your choosing. Weekends can be booked up months in advance. They give clear guidelines on what is required and it is easy to apply. Prices again depend on genre, but the maximum you will pay, at the time of this book going to print, is $16. This is for Romance and Mystery both of which are popular genres. I have used this service and I did notice a small increase in sales, which continued after the promotion finished.

Venture Galleries

With this site you are promoted as the book of the moment to the book of the moment club. This lasts for a period of seven days and costs $49.99. This means that you are able to take advantage of traffic for all seven days of the week, including weekends when traffic is highest. The application process is simple and easy to complete online.

Fire and Ice Book Promos

There are different ways in which you can advertise on this site - daily, weekly or monthly. The costs are obviously higher for a monthly slot. The daily advert costs just $5 and will be sent out as an email with only 9 other books. The 28 day VIP package costs $50 and has a number of features including a monthly competition for which the company buy your book. It is worth taking a look at this package to see what it has to offer. Please note, at the time of this book going to print all books for the promotion need to be priced $1.99 or below.

Before promoting your book on these sites it will need reviews. If you haven't got a minimum of 10 then most sites will not accept you for promotion. Some require more. Your book also needs at least a 3.5 star review average on Amazon. Most book promotion sites require your book to be available on multiple platforms e.g. Amazon, iBooks, Kobo etc. It also helps you to be accepted if you can be flexible with your timing. Make sure that you look at the requirements before submitting to make sure your book has the highest chance of being accepted.

This is just an example of some of the paid advertising sites that are out there. It is worth exploring others. A search on the internet will reveal many more. Before you go ahead with any paid promotion check that they have a number of subscribers written down on their site. That way you can make an informed choice as to whether it is worth paying out money.

Advertising on Social Media

Social Media sites are all free to use, but as I indicated earlier, they are also businesses. This means they need to make money in other ways. In order to encourage users to take out ads for their posts they throttle the reach of your posts. Advertising becomes the name of the game and this is how they make their money.

Facebook

You may have 2000 followers but only 4% of these will see any given post or tweet. This is the organic reach of your post. This is usually limited to people who have recently liked one of your posts so the same circle of people will be seeing each other's posts.

This means that in order to expand your reach you will need to use paid advertising. There are three ways in which you can do this.

The first is to **boost** an individual post. This can be done very cheaply depending on the number of people whom you would like to boost it to. This type of advertising merely shows the post to a larger number of people. It will contain a sponsored message.

The steps to boosting your post are simple:

1. Go to boost post in the corner of the post

2. Choose your audience and budget

3. Choose your payment method and budget.

There is some debate as to who will actually see these boosted posts. It used to be that it was difficult to target the right people. However, this seems to have improved and you can do slightly more finely tuned targeting. I have done a boosted post and I targeted my posts as follows:

Men and Women

Ages 18-65

UK, USA, Canada, Australia

I said I wanted to spend £7 on the boosted post over a period of 7 days. As I pay per click after £1 spent in a day the ad will stop being shown for that day.

It is worth trying a boosted post to see how it goes. My

advice would be to keep it for a new release or a special discount on your book. I used mine for the free download of my book to build my mailing list.

The next method is a **sponsored post**. This will be an ad created from a post. The ad will go to both fans and non-fans. The like button will show to non fans so they can like your page. It will contain the words promoted post.

The final, and most useful, method is a straight **advert**. This is more complex than the other two methods. You will develop your own ad using power editor. One important point, you can only use Power Editor if using Google Chrome. The advantage of using this method over the others is that it looks like any other post in the newsfeed. It will have promoted, but will also have its own URL. This means people can buy your books directly from the ad.

For all of these you set a budget for how much per day you are willing to spend. It is advisable to start low, say $5 per day. Also set the number of days you would like the ad to run for. It is important to make sure you do this or your costs could soon mount up.

If you are thinking of going down the advertising route then I would recommend that you complete Mark Dawson's excellent online course - Facebook Advertising for Authors. This is not cheap but it is worth the money to make sure that you are giving the ad its best chance of being seen. This takes you through the steps to make sure your advert is in the best place to receive click throughs and purchases.

Twitter

Twitter also provides a service to promote tweets in order to get them in front of a larger audience. In order to start a campaign and design you need to sign in to ads.twitter.com/getstarted. Once you have created an account click on the campaign you would like to use. The one you will use most often will be Website Clicks and Conversions.

You then follow these simple steps

1. Set up Your Campaign - give it a name and set start date and time

2. Select your audience

3. Set your budget - my advice would be to set a total budget for the life of the campaign. This way you will not overspend as the ad runs on for many weeks

4. Create your tweet - This should include the tweet, an image and the URL you are promoting

You can then either launch or save the tweet.

Mark Dawson also covers twitter in the course outlined above for Facebook. There is one module on Twitter Advertising.

Exercise

1. Block out half an hour of time in your diary.

2. Spend time exploring some of the different promotional sites.

3. Choose one and commit to taking out an advertising spot.

4. Boost one post using Facebook and monitor its effectiveness. You can do this with a spend of just £3.

Chapter 14

The Power of the Crowd

This is also known as social sharing and this should never be underestimated. Facebook and Twitter encourage this with their share and retweet functions respectively. However, social sharing is also so much more than this. It is also:

1. Word of mouth as readers tell their friends about the fantastic book they have just read

2. Reviews on Amazon and readers sharing those reviews

3. Readers emailing friends and telling them that they have just got to read this book

4. Fans telling their friends about your latest event on Facebook, Twitter, Google+ or any other social media site

5. Fans posting on your author page about how much they enjoyed your book

6. Contact from bloggers who would like to host you on their blogs

7. These blogs being shared and read by a wider audience than you can reach alone

The power of the crowd can expose you to many more potential readers and showcase you as a professional and well respected writer.

However, social sharing is not just about your own work being shared. It is important to be supportive of others and sharing their work where appropriate. This should not be done with any thought that you might get something in return, but because it is the right and helpful thing to do. It should be done because you want to.

Social sharing can happen in a number of ways. One of my friends was recently in hospital. The person in the bed opposite was reading one of my books, and my friend started a conversation about knowing me. The person in the next bed then heard about the books. Thus conversations are born and books are bought.

Here is another example of social sharing. I was doing a book signing in a shopping centre. I was setting up before the centre opened and one of the security guards came to chat to me. We had a conversation about the books and she bought one. All day people were then coming along to my table and saying Vicky sent me over. She says your books are great. They then bought a book. All because of a friendly conversation with a security guard. I wasn't trying to sell her my books, as I hadn't yet unpacked them. Yet, the net result was I got several sales.

You are probably realising that social sharing cannot be bought. Yet, it is possibly the most powerful form of advertising that can be used. The power of the crowd is exponentially greater than all the individual sales you make. I can't advise you how to make this happen, I can only say be nice to people. Talk to them as people not potential customers. Take an interest in them. They may buy then, they may buy in the future, or they may not buy at all. However, you can bet your bottom dollar they will be telling their friends they met an author and how friendly he/she was. This may be what gets you the sale.

Social sharing will come when you treat people as you would like to be treated yourself. When you are supportive of other authors and engage with readers. This engagement does not mean answering every review you get on Amazon or anywhere else. In fact most writers advise you never to respond to amazon reviews whether good or bad. They are one reader's perspective on your work and your book. They are entitled to review about that perspective no matter what their thoughts are.

Social sharing is also about the way you behave on social media. We all share our thoughts and feelings on social media each day. Friends, family, fans and prospective fans can see these unless you have your account locked down tighter than the vaults in the bank of England. They will make assumptions based on what you say. It is important to be positive in the way you come across. Even when handling criticisms in social media comments, remain polite and do not get into an argument. On the whole it is better to ignore negative or inflammatory comments rather than start a flame war. Handle yourself pleasantly and professionally at all times. I appreciate most authors reading this will already know, and act, like that. However, it can be so easy to react badly when faced with criticism.

One of the best ways to gain influence on social media is to start following others. Share their posts, retweet their tweets, comment on blogs or their posts. They may then follow or friend you and a relationship can start to develop. One caveat, do not do this to the point of creepiness. This may get you noticed in the wrong way. Once you build up a relationship with others they are more likely to be supportive of you and help you to share your posts and work.

However, the power of the crowd is so much more than social sharing. It is also about working together with other authors. This can be done in a number of ways:

1. Joint book signings

2. Joint speaking engagements

3. Interviewing each other or hosting each other on blogs

4. Providing support and advice

In conjunction with a local bookshop I organized a four author event called, Local Authors Live. Each author represented a different genre - crime, historical saga, young adult and children's. We spent four hours in the shop using a joint table for our books. During this time we chatted with customers and told them about not only our books, but also those of the other authors. This can work well if all the authors are invested in selling all of the books. It is quite a simple premise. When a customer approaches and starts to look at books, simply ask them what type of books they are looking for that day. They may be looking for a present for a grandchild, or looking for a crime book to take on holiday with them. Authors should be prepared to talk about all the books placed on the tables. No one should be in competition with anyone else.

Joint author talks can also be fun. This can be in the form of a chat between two authors or the authors could question each other about their work. It is a matter of identifying another author and then agreeing on the process. However, remember the public are involved and their questions can be enlightening. I will say no more about that part of promotion.

Exercise

1. Identify one key influencer in your genre who is on one of the social media sites.

2. Read their posts and follow their page or tweets.

3. Observe how they interact with others.

4. Join in the conversation once you have an idea of how they work.

5. Spend ten minutes a day updating your social media. This does not need to be all at once but can be just a couple of minutes every now and then. Share things about what you are doing and one post about your books.

Chapter 15

Keywords

Keywords are used online to increase your book's visibility and allow it to rank higher in the search engines of online shops. For most writers this will mean Amazon. A quick search of the Internet will give you thousands of articles on this topic. They all agree it is worth spending time to get your keywords right. This is one of the main ways in which readers can discover your books. The beauty of this is that it can be done from your computer sitting at home.

When you are deciding on keywords you should be thinking like a customer. What would a customer search for if they were looking for a particular genre of book. As a note keywords cannot include your title, or subjective claims about quality such as bestselling. Amazon has been clamping down on these recently and has been removing them. You can't add something like new either as this is only a temporary. Amazon recommends that you use the following guide

Setting

Themes

Character roles

Character types

Story tone

So taking these individually you could use:

Setting - Scottish, English, British, International, Contemporary Scotland, Jacobean Scotland

Okay I'm Scottish so bear with me here.

Themes - revenge, psychological, coming of age

Character roles - strong female lead, bullied teenager,

Character types - single mother, single father, transgender teen, harried detective

Story tone - gritty, realistic, dystopian

These are just examples from both Amazon and myself. I am sure as writers you will be able to think of many more.

You can also use a combination of these to make long tailed keywords. Amazon will allow you to use phrases. So for my crime books I could use:

Gritty Scottish Crime

Gritty Crime Contemporary Scotland

Tartan Noir - This is a style of Scottish Crime Writing and people will actually search using this term. It is worth exploring if there are any such titles that fit your genre or country

If you are traditionally published then your publisher will set the key words. If you are an indie author you can change the keywords as often as you want. If your books are selling well then leave the keywords be. If you would like to boost sales then it is worth exploring different keywords.

I will say one more thing about keywords. Amazon only allows for a certain number of words/characters in this section. Some authors try to get round this by stuffing as many keywords into the title as possible. They do this in brackets after the main title. I would advise you not to do this for a number of reasons. It looks both unprofessional and, I think, a little desperate. You will have spent time choosing your title and ensuring it shows your book in its best light. Why ruin it by including a lot of random words at the end.

This is one area it is worth taking time over. If you know other authors ask them what key words they use. Do searches for different keywords and see what comes up on Google, Bing or any other search engine. If it is Aamzon which comes up first then it is probably a keyword which Amazon uses. This can be one of the best ways to get your books noticed, so not something to take lightly.

Exercise

1. Brainstorm some keywords for your books.
2. If you would like more traction on Amazon check your keywords. Do they adequately convey the tone and genre of your book?
3. If you are an indie author change your keywords for one book on Amazon.
4. If you are not yet published start to think about what keywords would suit books in your genre. Keep these in a notebook for your book. Add to them as more come to mind.

Chapter 16

Author Pages

Your author page, whatever platform may hold it, is your window to the outside world. It is the space for you to showcase yourself and your books. It is worthwhile spending time, energy and resources on this aspect of your marketing. It is also one of the easiest parts of your Power Packed Marketing strategy to get right.

Make this the best page it can be. Spend money on a professional photo. This is not the time for that photo taken on a day trip to Blackpool. This is the opportunity for you to show yourself as a professional and someone who pays attention to detail. Your author bio should also reflect you as both a person and a professional.

If considering your Amazon Author page all published books should be on this page with covers, and blurbs, which catch the reader's attention. Your branding will show here in glorious technicolour detail. This is one of the reasons why it is worth investing in branding your covers over all the books in a series. This needs to be updated the minute a new book is available.

Make sure that the author page on your website is up to date and contains all the books which you have written. It is so easy to forget this part of the website when in the throes of launching a book. I am saying this from experience. My author bio was still saying I only had one book when I actually had 3 out. If you are an indie author you will be able to change your Amazon Author Page as well by going to Amazon author central.

Exercise

1. Check your Amazon Author page. Is it showing you in the best light?

2. Make any required changes.

3. Do the same for your website author page.

4. If you are available for talks, workshops or book signings add this to you website author page.

Chapter 17

Podcasting

As a writer there are a number of ways in which podcasts can help you market your book. These are:

1. Listening to podcasts on book marketing by industry experts

2. Appearing as a guest on established podcasts

3. Podcasters talking about you and your books

4. Starting up and maintaining your own podcast

Listening to Podcasts

There are a number of excellent podcasts out there, both on marketing and writing. The ones I have found to be most useful, and which I would highly recommend are:

The Creative Penn
http://www.thecreativepenn.com/podcasts/

The Sell More Books Show
http://sellmorebooksshow.com

The Creative Writer's Toolbelt   http://ajc-cwt-001.podomatic.com

The Alliance of Independent Authors
https://itunes.apple.com/us/podcast/alli-author-advice-centre/id1080135033?mt=2

Author Strong   http://authorstrong.com/podcast/

These are all podcasts which have been running for some time. They are also by industry experts who have a lot of experience in the field of writing and marketing. You can subscribe to each of these on iTunes or from the relevant websites. I listen to podcasts when I am in the car. Not only does this pass the time but allows me to learn at the same time. I have gained a lot of valuable insight from these podcasts.

There are also podcasters who interview writers in different genres. It is worth exploring these to find out what podcasts are available in your genre. I am subscribed to one called Crime Writers On … You may also find podcasts for your local area. Whatever you come up with I am sure there is a podcast out there for it.

Guesting on a Podcast

All of these podcasts have featured guests. This is a chance to hear from an industry expert in a particular niche. I have guested on one podcast, The Creative Writers Toolbelt, run by Andrew Chamberlain. This is an excellent podcast which talks mainly about writing. Andrew is a creative writing tutor and his advice is sound and helpful. It was a thrill to be invited along. Andrew sent me the questions in advance. The recording was simply done through Skype. I moved into the dining room with my laptop for the recording. This is because my office used to be a garage so echoes a little. The sound was clearer in the carpeted and well insulated, dining room. This is something to think about if you are invited to be a guest.

It is important to prepare for the interview and to jot down notes on what you might say. Don't stick rigidly to this though, or you may come across as wooden. It can be a lot of fun so relax and enjoy yourself. It is also useful to know a bit about the person who has invited you and the podcast on which you will be guesting.

After the podcast is finished you may be sent a raw copy to listen to before it goes out. This is your chance to ask for something to be taken out if you do not like the sound of it. Obviously only use this if you have to otherwise the podcast may sound strange.

The beauty of this is that not only is your podcast on

iTunes but you can share it elsewhere. I have uploaded it to my own website and it is also on a number of other websites. This spreads the word far and wide and the reach rises exponentially with every share.

Social Sharing through Podcasts

Although you may not be invited to guest on a podcast, the podcasters may sometimes talk about you and your books. On the Sell More Book Show podcast you have an opportunity to support the show on Patreon. If you do this then they will mention your book on the show. You may also find that podcasters talk about books by other authors if they like the books. You obviously cannot manufacture this but if it happens it is more valuable than a priceless jewel.

Setting up Your Own Podcast

This is slightly more complex than the other methods as it involves time, expense and some level of expertise. However, these steps can be learned and it is worth the investment to do so. But why? Why would you want to do a podcast in the first place? There are a number of reasons:

1. You have an idea for a subject

2. It's a way of helping others

3. You can build your brand name

4. It is fun

In order to start a podcast you will need:

1. A good quality microphone. This is important because sound quality is important for the quality of the completed product

2. A quiet space in which to record

3. A recording device such as a PC or Mac

4. Recording software. Andrew Chamberlain recommends audacity.com

5. Podcast host to store your podcast. Andrew Chamberlain outlines some which are available including Podomatic, Libsyn, Archive.org, Ourmedia.org, and Podbean. These will give you an RSS feed to use in the places that listeners will find you. The most famous one of these is iTunes but you can also put it on your own website.

You will need to think about how you will start and end your podcast. This should be the same in every podcast. You may want to have a jingle as well. This will identify your podcast to your listeners. To get an idea of ways in which to start and end your podcasts, listen to some. You may want to start with the podcasts I have outlined above.

Audacity will not only allow you to record your interview but will allow you to clip out the bits that you don't want such as silences. It is important to ensure that your podcast is professionally done and sounds good.

I know there are people who do not like Podcasts and you may be one of them. I appreciate where you are coming from here. We all like different things. I would ask you to think back to what I said at the beginning of the book. It is what the reader enjoys that is important. You need to meet your readers at the place they are at. If you ignore podcasts in their entirety you are ignoring those who listen to podcasts and will hear about your books in that way. You may not want to set up your own Podcast but think about being a guest on one.

Exercise

1. Choose one of the recommended podcasts and listen to some of the episodes.

2. Do a search for Podcasts which might interest you. Listen to one episode of a few of them.

3. Contact one person who runs a podcast and ask them if they are looking for guests.

Chapter 18

Public Speaking

Speaking engagements are a way of meeting new readers, getting your name out there and selling books. Again, they can also be a lot of fun. How do we find these speaking engagements? I have done this in a number of ways. Obviously, these have worked for me, but you may have to think of your own methods. You can use my ideas as a springboard for the public speaking part of your Power Packed Marketing Plan.

Contact your local librarians and explain that you are a local author. Ask them if they would like you to do a talk? They may say that you will have to contact the head librarian for the region. Others have the authority to book you in themselves. Be ready to explain what your book is about and why it would fit in with that particular library. For example, the main detective in my book, DI Shona McKenzie, lives in Broughty Ferry. Therefore, Broughty Ferry library were keen for me to do a talk. My books are popular in Dundee libraries, so I have managed to do an Author talk in several of these. One important thing to remember, if you give a number of talks in a small geographical area you must ensure that you vary your talks. Whilst on the whole the audience will be different, there may be some who come to everything. To be honest, I have found that this makes sure that I keep the talks fresh and lively. This will come across to anyone who is in the audience and you will sound more natural.

Local groups are often looking for speakers. These include Rotary clubs, women's groups, educational groups, writer's groups and the Women's Institute among many others. I have found that when I'm doing book signings I have been approached by people looking for speakers for their groups. The library and bookshops have also advised people to contact me when they're looking for speakers. When local organisations start to recognise that you are a competent and confident speaker they recommend you to others. You are free to contact as many groups as you feel is appropriate.

There is much discussion and debate at the moment regarding payment for public speaking and events. I agree that authors should be paid for their time in preparing for the event and the event itself. However, I made the decision that I will talk at libraries and schools for free. My reasoning behind this is that very often these institutions have very little budget for visiting speakers. I do, however, ask if I'm allowed to sell books. The answer has always been yes and I have always sold enough books to make it worth my while attending the events. You will need to make the decision as to what is acceptable for you.

When I do talks for public groups I do expect payment. This has never been a problem and all groups have been willing to pay. I also sell books at these events.

One thing to consider, although you can sell books at author events, it is not guaranteed that you will sell many or even any. I use them as a promotional tool as well as an opportunity to sell books. Take postcards and business cards along and hand these out to participants. You may sell books down the line either through bookshops, your website or online stores.

Another way, which you can support others whilst getting your name known, and selling books, are writers' workshops or courses. I have been asked to run individual workshops and a short beginners course. It is worth looking out for opportunities such as these. Not only will you be helping local community but it is also a chance for you to sell books. Again, the focus is not on selling your books but in supporting others to move their own writing forward.

Exercise

1. Identify groups in your local area who may be looking for speakers.

2. Approach one of these groups and ask them if they would be interested in you doing a talk.

3. Approach your local library and discuss the possibility of your doing an author talk.

Chapter 19

Short Tail Versus Long Tail Promotion

In a nutshell short tailed marketing is reducing the price of an item and seeing a spike in sales. It is also releasing a new book and seeing a spike in sales. Long tailed marketing is reducing the price of one item in order to sell the more lucrative items in your store. Supermarkets employ this extremely successfully with their loss leaders. For authors this may mean selling the first book in the series at a reduced price in order to sell the other books in the series at full price. It could also mean reducing the price of the book briefly for a paid promotion in the expectation that the book will continue to sell after the promotion is finished. This may happen because the paid promotion drives the book up the charts. It is then in a good position to be noticed by potential readers.

Short tailed promotion will hopefully give you a spike in sales on the day of the promotion. However as an author the long tail effect is most important for long-term success. This will provide steady income throughout the life of your books. This involves long-term promotion of your books.

There is a strong argument that having one book in a series perma-free can boost sales of the remaining books in the series. If you have several books under your belt this may be something that you would like to try. I have not yet tried this, however I am told that many authors have used this successfully.

If you feel that you do not have enough books out as yet to go for a perma-free book, reducing the price of the first in series can also work. You will need to work out the price to which you are willing to lower your book. There is a strong argument for this price point to be £0.99 or $0.99. It may be worth trying out different price points to see which works for you. One point of note, this may only be possible if you are an indie author. Those who are traditionally published may not have the flexibility to adjust prices.

It may also be worth looking at having different books on promotion at different times. Bryan Cohen in his successful Sell More Books Show podcast puts forward the thought that as one book comes off promotion put the next one on. This can cause a ripple effect which can lead to long term book sales.

Chapter 20

Where in the World

Unless you are living at the bottom of the ocean you will probably have noticed there are numerous versions of books - hardback, paperback, ebook and audiobook. You can buy books from many different places. Traditionally books were purchased from chain and Indie bookshops. For several years now you have been able to download books straight to ereaders from stores such as Amazon, Kobo, iBooks, Nook, Google Play and Smashwords. You can also get them from subscription services such as Oyster and Scribd. Libraries are choc full of books in all formats and these can be borrowed for free. Supermarkets stock books and airports have vending machines for books. Readers can also buy books from Author and Publisher websites. In fact they are everywhere. Why is she telling me this I hear you ask? I already know that.

This catalogue is important for one very good reason. If you want to sell books you should be in as many of these as you possibly can. Okay, the airport vending machine version might be a bit trickier but the rest are up for grabs.

Firstly make sure that your books are out in all formats. Whilst many readers are now turning to ebooks there are still an equal number who will read physical books. Many readers bounce between both. I know I certainly do. People now lead busy lives and find themselves driving long distances. Many of these will listen to audiobooks to pass the time. At the time of writing this book I am currently in the process of working with a narrator to get my first DI Shona McKenzie book, Killer's Countdown, narrated for audiobook. If you have a traditional publisher they will deal with the audiobook production. If you are an Indie author then you will need to deal with Amazon ACX to get your book narrated and published as an audiobook. The process for this could be a whole book in itself. I will not be discussing this in here and would advise you to research it carefully before going ahead. I will say one last thing about audio books. There are two ways in which you can work with a narrator. The first is to pay them up front. This way all profits from the book will belong to you. If you wish to go down this route then you will need to make sure you have the upfront cost which can run to thousands of pounds. The other way is to profit share through ACX. This way Amazon or Audible will pay the narrator and the author half of the profits of the audiobook. This will be for the lifetime of the book.

Once your book is available in all formats then my advice would be to go for as wide a distribution as possible. If you are an Indie author you will have total control over this. Some authors argue that it is better to stay exclusive to Amazon. This means that Amazon will advertise and promote your book more freely. You also receive larger royalties per book in all markets. However, my advice would be to cast your net wide. This allows you to grow a readership on other platforms and reach a wider audience. You will obviously need to decide which method will work for you. It may be that you would like to try one of your books in KDP select (Amazon exclusivity) for a period of 90 days. This is the minimum length of time you can do this for. During this time you can reduce the price, or even make the book free, on selected days. During this time Amazon will promote your book.

Another aspect of marketing concerns the title of this chapter - Where in the World? The answer to that should be everywhere it is possible to be. Ebooks are available in most countries in the world so that is not an issue. Pricing, however, is an issue. Different countries will sustain different pricing points. Books can be more expensive in Australia and Canada as readers are used to this. However, if you wish to sell books in India, you will need to price your books at 60 India Rupees. This is because readers in India are accustomed to buying books more cheaply. At the time of writing, ebooks are becoming more popular in India due, for the most part, to the rise in mobile phone use. I would advise you to think carefully about the price of your book in different markets. It is worth doing some research in this area.

Distributing paperback books worldwide is more difficult. If your books are available in Paperback or Hardback on Amazon they will be available for purchase in:

UK

USA

Canada

France

Germany

Spain

India

Brazil

Mexico

International distribution to other countries may be one area where you wish to seek an agent to take this further.

There is also a ripple effect from having books both locally and internationally. You may start off by selling books locally, particularly if your books are set in your local area. If those readers like the books they will tell their friends about it and this moves nationally. They then have friends living abroad and they tell them. They tell their friends and so an international readership is born. We are now living globally and there will be a global response to your books. In fact everyone expects to be able to buy your books everywhere. I have had requests from Lesotho as to where my books can be bought. At the time of writing I have sold books in UK, USA, Spain, France, Germany, Netherlands, Canada,

New Zealand and Australia. I am working on being sold in every country in the world.

Whatever you do, do not miss, or turn down an opportunity to get your book in front of readers. Seize all of the above opportunities and use them in a way which will work for you. You do not need to do all of this all at once, but wait for the right opportunity. Killer's Countdown has been out for 18 months and I am only now considering an audiobook.

Exercise

1. Do an audit of where your book is available for both vendors and geographically.

2. If you are lacking in any area consider if this is somewhere you would like your book to be.

3. Write an action plan to ensure your book is available in all locations.

Chapter 21

What Now

I am sure by now your head is spinning with all the things you feel you have to do to sell your books. You may be feeling overwhelmed and thinking, this is not for me. It is important to remember that even doing a few of these steps will help you to sell more books. I cannot promise you that you will be a multimillion selling author, but I can promise you that it will get you and your books noticed. Getting noticed in the right way will bring sales along with it.

The old saying, any journey starts with a single step is equally true for marketing. This step for you is to choose one thing you feel you could do from this book. Focus on that and start to do it today. Brainstorm ways that it could work for you.

One thing that I did was buying a yearly planner for my wall. I then plot down on there what I am doing for marketing for each week of the year. Some weeks I may have several things on the plan. Other weeks I may only have one. However, I can see at a glance where I am going with my marketing. If you do this and mark done just one marketing activity per week that is still 52 opportunities to market your book.

Writing, and publishing, more books should be a large part of your marketing plan. In fact it should be the biggest part. The number one way to market your books is to write more books. Very often, before buying a book, readers will look to see how many other books the author has written. If a reader enjoys an author's book they will often go and buy several others immediately after finishing it. Books sell books. Hence the reason I am currently investing my paid advertising in the first book in my series.

This leads me on to the back matter in your book. This should have the names of all the other books you have written. In the case of digital books it should also have links to buy these books. You may also want to include the first chapter of your next book. This is also an incentive to make sure that the opening chapters of your next book are dynamic and attention grabbing. Make them end on a cliffhanger so readers want to know what happens next.

The most important thing to remember about marketing is that it is fun. If you are dreading everything you do in terms of marketing then it is time to rethink your marketing strategy. Yes, you may need to step outside your comfort zone. That is inevitable. However, you should not be miserable in the process. Use this book to guide you and to give you inspiration. Decide which of these methods you will use, if any. Use it to give form to your own ideas and develop your own individual

Power Packed Marketing Plan.

By now you should have, at the very least, a basic marketing plan in place. You may now have a detailed plan and be keen and ready to get cracking. Whatever stage you are at I would encourage you to take steps to market your book now. I wish you all the very best with your books and your sales.

Chapter 22

Recommended Resources

There are a number of excellent resources to help you to develop your marketing plan. These are some, which I found highly valuable. Please note these are under categories and in alphabetical order. The order they are in does not indicate any one of these being any better than the others. These are all excellent resources in their own right. They are not all overtly, marketing books, but I believe they all have value within the marketing process.

Books

Caballo, Frances, (2012), **Social Media Just for Writers**: The Best Online Marketing Tips for Selling Your Books, Act Communications

As the name suggests this is a book on social media for writing. It is jam packed full of useful information and recommended resources and links.

Carvill, Michelle and Taylor, David, (2013), **The Business of Being Social**, Crimson Publishing Ltd.

This book takes you through the process of using social media marketing in a small business setting.

Conlon, Ciara, (2016), **Productivity for Dummies**, John Wiley and Sons

As writers, one of the main objections to marketing is that we do not have time. This book will help you to look at how you manage your time and work towards using it more effectively.

Corder, Honoree, (2015**), Prosperity for Writers**: A Writer's Guide to Creating Abundance, Honoree Enterprises Publishing

This takes a different approach in that it helps you to change your mindset about marketing.

Hall, Rayne, (2014), **Twitter for Writers**, Rayne Hall

This is an excellent How To book about using Twitter to support your marketing as a writer.

Hardy, Darren, (2012), **The Compound Effect**: Jumpstart your income, your life, your success, DA Capo Press

Again this book will help you to change your mindset about the way you approach marketing and making money.

Lancaster, Paul and Shenck Barabara, (2014), **Small Business Marketing for Dummies**, John Wiley and Sons

Choc full of good advice about the basics of marketing.

Lansky, D'vorah, (2015), **Productivity Action Guide for Authors**, Vibrant Marketing Publications

This book is part of a longer online course. However, it is full of exercises which will help you to manage your marketing and your timekeeping.

Montano, Liberty, (2011), **Novel Blogging**: A Writer's Guide to Blogging, Createspace Independent Publishing

This is exactly what it says in the title. It is about using blogging if you are a writer.

Penn Joanna, (2015), **How to make a Living with your Writing**, Createspace Independent Publishing

Jam packed full of advice on how to make a living from writing your books.

Schaeffer, Mark W., (2012), **The Tao of Twitter**: Changing your life and business 140 characters at a time, McGraw Hill

This is possibly the best book on Twitter I have read. It is not specifically for writers but will help you to understand and use Twitter to your greater advantage.

Sutherland, Ian H., (2015), **Advanced Twitter Strategies for Authors**, Brookmans Books

Another useful guide to using Twitter.

Syme, Chris, (2016), **SMART Social Media for Authors**, Createspace Independent Publishing

At the time of writing this is the most up to date, and useful, book on using social media for marketing your books.

Young, Debbie, (2015), **Sell Your Books**: A Book Promotion Handbook for the Self-Published or Indie Authors, Silverwood Books

Takes you through the process of book marketing.

Websites

The Creative Penn   http://www.thecreativepenn.com

The Sell More Books Show
http://sellmorebooksshow.com

Jessica Bell   http://www.jessicabellauthor.com

Author Strong   http://authorstrong.com

WENDY H. JONES

Wendy H. Jones is the author of the highly successful crime series The DI Shona McKenzie Mysteries. After having a career in the Military she moved into Academia, where she wrote for academic publications and textbooks. She has had extensive marketing training throughout her career. After a period of illness she moved back to her native Scotland where she settled in Dundee. This led to her career as an author. She loves writing but has embraced the marketing aspect of the role with enthusiasm. On meeting people they often greet her with, "I saw you at …. You're everywhere." This is possibly quite true, as she loves meeting readers and talking about both books and writing. She is also a skilled public speaker, having presented at a number of International Conferences, and has developed this to include presentations on marketing your books.

FIND OUT MORE

Website: http://www.wendyhjones.com

Full list of links: http://about.me/WendyHJones

Twitter: https://twitter.com/WendyHJones

Pinterest: http://www.pinterest.com/wjones64/

More Books by Wendy H. Jones

The DI Shona McKenzie Mysteries

Killer's Countdown
Killer's Craft
Killer's Cross
KIller's Cut - To be released 18th April, 2016

Lightning Source UK Ltd.
Milton Keynes UK
UKOW02f1021110417
298859UK00001B/65/P